How to Be
Popular

# How to Be Popular

## EVERYTHING YOU NEED TO KNOW, AND MORE!

**Jennifer McKnight-Trontz**

**CHRONICLE BOOKS**

SAN FRANCISCO

## For Esme

*Thanks to Chronicle Books for giving me the opportunity to work with them again. Special thanks to my editor, Steve Mockus, without whose continuous support these past few years, I would have had to get a real job. And thank you to all the people who created the wonderful material featured in this book. Their efforts over the years have undoubtedly helped many reach popularity. If only it were simple.*

Pages 120–123 constitute a continuation of the copyright page. Every effort has been made to trace the ownership of all copyrighted material included in this volume. Any errors that may have occurred are inadvertent and will be corrected in subsequent editions, provided notification is sent to the publisher.

Library of Congress Cataloging-in-Publication Data available.

ISBN 0-8118-3570-7

Manufactured in China

Book design by Jennifer McKnight-Trontz
Cover design by Benjamin Shaykin
Cover illustration courtesy CSA Images

Distributed in Canada by Raincoast Books
9050 Shaughnessy Street
Vancouver, British Columbia V6P 6E5

10 9 8 7 6 5 4 3

Chronicle Books LLC
85 Second Street
San Francisco, California 94105

www.chroniclebooks.com

# Contents

*An Introduction to Popularity*

# Do you want to be popular?

O F COURSE you want to be popular. Everyone does. Everyone likes *to be liked.*

Then what's the secret of popularity? What will make you *likable?* And how do you "get that way"?

You know the secret of popularity isn't beauty or money or a bundle of brains, because you see plenty of examples to the contrary.

There's Jane. She isn't beautiful. In fact, she's almost homely in looks. But Jane's popularity plus. Why? Because she has a friendly smile for everyone and she's always ready to pitch in and help get a job done.

Ted helps support his family, so he doesn't have much spending money. But Ted's well-mannered, considerate of others, interested in everything that goes on at school, and always in a good humor. He's Number 1 on the Date Parade.

Phoebe isn't a brain-box but she's a good dancer and a good conversationalist and, when she talks, she "makes sense." Phoebe gets around.

## IS IT IMPORTANT TO BE POPULAR?
## DOES IT REALLY MATTER IN THE LONG RUN?

### IT MATTERS VERY MUCH

Is it important to be popular? Does it really matter in the long run?

The answer is "yes" to both of these questions for the very basic reason that everyone wants to be liked. It's essential to morale.

We all need to know that people care about us. What is the value of good news if we've no one to share it with? And think how much more tragic sad news becomes when there's no one to offer sympathy.

Popularity provides these very necessary reassurances.

EST ATHLETE
MOST
POPULAR
MOST VERSATILE

# What does it take?

**One can never improve himself until he honestly admits that there are areas which need improvement.** Most of us have at least a few personality defects (characteristics or mannerisms) which lower our popularity rating. It is only when we face this fact honestly that we can profit from the help and suggestions of others.

There are several ways in which you may determine your weaknesses. The way other people feel about you is a good thermometer of your acceptance and popularity. Do others ignore you? Do they simply tolerate you when you're around? Do they make "catty" remarks in your presence? Do they include you in their plans and activities? You can tell pretty well whether you are liked or not.

# Take a good look at those who are popular

**Where do they go?**

**What do they do?**

**Try to be like them.**

Popularity is like a tree. It has a trunk and branches. The stronger the trunk is, the more impressive the main branches are, and the more numerous the little branches are.

# Mirror, Mirror

. . . are you the fairest one of all?

# Beautiful

▶ *Science Makes You More Beautiful*

Being beautiful, too, has become easier with the advance of science. Our clothes are finer, better made, more lasting with new miracle fabrics—nylon, dacron, orlon, dynel, acrilon, vicara, milium, tycora, fiberglas, lastex. (The fine silk of yesterday's princesses is just ordinary.) Machinery has made fine hosiery, fine dressmaking, fine footwear available in endless variety for every budget.

Technology and chemistry work, too, on the skin and hair. Science offers:

Simple, painless plastic surgery for the scarred.
New colors and tints for your hair, comparatively inexpensive.
Synthetic perfumes indistinguishable from famous fragrances.
Hormone face creams that keep skin young and clear.
Home-permanent kits.
Dry-skin softeners.
Hair sprays that keep your set in place.
Hair sprays that will change the color of your hair completely in
    five minutes, and remain till washed out.
Non-allergenic cosmetics.

NO!

yes

## *Every Day:*

1. Shower
2. Deodorant
3. Teeth brushed
4. Hair care
5. Clean underclothes
6. Shoes shined
7. Nails clean, filed
8. Posture perfect
9. Bed made, room straightened
10. Colors blended
11. Accessories right

Give yourself a sun-tan tattoo. Cut out a small diamond or flower shape and paste it on your shoulder when you sun bathe. Small beauty spots are best; hearts are fun. Avoid large shapes or complicated designs—you don't want to look like a sailor!

# *Physical Traits*

The following physical traits are considered good by the majority of people:

**HEIGHT:** average for the sex to slightly above.

**WEIGHT:** average and in standard proportion to height.

**COMPLEXION:** medium blond or medium brunette; skin of healthy color.

**HEALTH:** the nearer perfect, the better.

**MOVEMENTS:** slightly more important in women than men.

**STRENGTH:** the greater the better in men; capacity for endurance in both men and women.

**CLOTHES:** becoming to the person, appropriate for the season and the occasion. This item applies to men and women alike.

32

# The Hippest Closet in Town

Pick out your clothes, including underthings, the night before, and avoid the frantic morning madness. You'll feel (and look) much more together than you could via last-minute grabbing and matching.

Short girls will look better in those great one-piece jumpsuits instead of figure-splitting pants-and-tops combos.

Then, vertical stripes are the best pattern for the girls who want thinner looking legs.

Stretch your wardrobe by buying mix-and-match separates. It also helps if you select a basic color scheme and stick to it.

Double your fashion dollars. Look for the pants set with top that can double as a mini.

# Stay hip, but avoid fads

*Research shows that if you wear certain colors, you will appear to be in a bright, cheery mood, and if you appear to be in a bright, cheery mood most of the time, you are much more likely to be liked by both men and women.*

*Tired of counting those necessary one hundred brush strokes for your hair? Just flick on your radio or phono and brush for the entire length of any pop tune. That'll do it.*

# A Breath Away from Popularity

**IF YOU WANT TO BREATHE EASY,** watch what you eat before you plunge into a social occasion. Avoid garlic, onions, scallions and radishes.

More than that, check breath by brushing after meals, and if you have doubts, swish around some mouthwash.

If bad breath is a frequent problem, see your dentist (it could be a tooth infection) or your doctor (an upset stomach might be to blame).

Front view of upper- and lower-middle-class men walking.
Upper-middle-class man (left)—shoulders straight,
arms in toward body, walk almost military. Lower-
middle-class man (right)—shoulders and body roll,
arms are throwing out, hips swing.

# MODELING ROUTINES

Have you ever watched a Fashion Show and marveled that the models knew just the right time to turn, or stand still, or how far to walk to the right, or to the left? Well, each pivot and stance is a part of a routine or pattern which she has studied and practiced. She knows exactly where to go, and what to do, before she ever faces an audience. This "know-how" is the secret of her stage presence. She is confident because she is sure. You too, can acquire the graceful, natural look of a model by practicing the following four routines, which are the basic patterns used by famous models for "showing clothes".

The patterns in which you walk, stand and pivot, will draw capital letters "T", "Y", "V" and inverted "V" on the stage or floor.

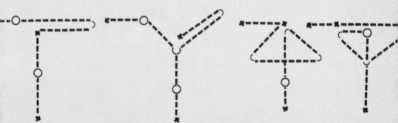

KEY  ◯ FULL PIVOT  ∪ HALF PIVOT  ( QUARTER PIVOT  ✖ STANCE

Posture

# Eye magic

**YOUR EYES ARE THE MOST IMPORTANT PART OF YOUR FACE,**
and perhaps the most important feature of your physical
appearance. Beautiful, expressive eyes can be your greatest
asset. Cultivate a pleasing eye personality (avoid angry or
dull expressions), then learn to look people in the eye. They
will be hypnotized into returning your glance. Later, they may
not even remember what you look like, but your beautiful
eyes will have captivated them.

The
Magnetic
You

. . . how to attract!

## *Have Confidence in Yourself*

If you want to get in the social swim, there's just one sure way to go about it. Take the plunge.

Be ready and set, then go.

There's just one asset you need to float along with the social tide. It's confidence. When you know appearance and personality are pleasing, you've got it. You're ready and set, so go! go! go!

# *Popular People Are Enthusiastic!*

**Assets of Enthusiasm:**

Enthusiasm wins respect.

It stimulates followers by getting them to think.

It's a calculated invasion of the "likes" of other people.

It's a role played to achieve an end.

It inspires confidence.

It's a compelling step away from mediocrity.

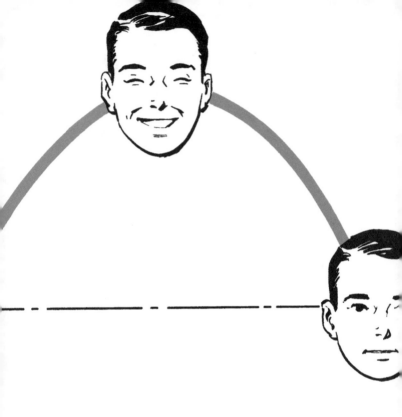

*Don't you love to be around a happy person?*
*You get a "lift" from those who radiate sunshine.*
*They are popular with you, aren't they?*

# HAPPINESS

Are you charming?

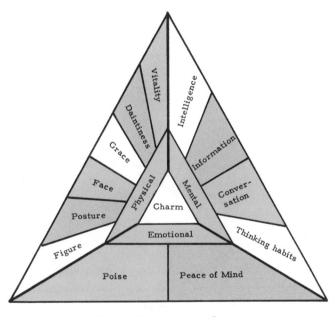

TESTING YOURSELF FOR CHARM

*Bad manners can make
you very unpopular*

# Humility

The antonym for humility is arrogance. The conceited, puffed-up-with-pride type personality never makes the list of popular people. We sometimes hear it said of a person that his or her humility is showing. In other words, conceit oozes out in subtle, and often not-so-subtle, ways. Humble courtesy is an important quality for anyone who wants to be liked by others.

# *Introvert or Extrovert?*

Here is a short test that may help you to determine whether you tend to be an extrovert or introvert.

Do you enjoy being with people?
Yes ( ) No ( )

Do you show genuine interest in conversation? Yes ( ) No ( )

Do you like to do things for people?
Yes ( ) No ( )

Do you like to be in charge of committees? Yes ( ) No ( )

Do you laugh easily at a joke?
Yes ( ) No ( )

Can you take criticism lightly?
Yes ( ) No ( )

Are you at ease in new situations?
Yes ( ) No ( )

If most of your answers are *yes,* you probably tend to be an extrovert; if most are *no,* you likely tend to be an introvert. Maybe your answers are about evenly divided, so that would make you an ambivert. When you are around people who are not aggressive, you may be extroverted, and vice versa.

# Popularity at the Office

**AVOID THESE HARMFUL
PERSONALITY TRAITS:**

1. sorrow
2. anger
3. hate
4. fear, terror
5. jealousy
6. worry
7. pessimism

## DEPENDABILITY

Be a person on whom others can depend.

Be meticulous in the payment of all obligations.

Be on time for every party and "date."

Be one of those persons who are always on hand whenever someone needs a friend.

Do not go through life leaning on others, but let others lean on you and you will be known far and wide as kindly, generous, and altogether a splendid sort of person.

That is the kind of charm that is permanent. That will give you a poise that is unassailable. That will make you popular.

**YOUR VOICE IS YOUR INSTRUMENT** you use to tell people what you're like, so what you say and how you say it can win friends and fans or lose them.

If possible, make tape recordings. Note your shortcomings and try to overcome them.

You certainly do *not* need an over-cultivated,

*English*-sounding accent to make your points!

| | |
|---|---|
| *potato* | pṓ-tā′tō (not *p* |
| *quinine* | kwī′nīn; kwĭ-r |
| *respite* | rĕs′pĭt (not *re* |
| *route* | rō͞ot (generally |
| *suggest* | sŭg-jĕst′ (not |
| *theater* | thē′*a*-tẽr (not |
| *veterinary* | vĕt′ẽr-ĭ-nā̇-rĭ |
| *vitamin* | vī′tȧ-mĭn; vĭt′*a* |

*r Speech*

*tater*)

*ı′; -nīn′*

*bite′*)

ccepted except in special cases)

*jjest*)

*eeay′ter*)

also, -mīn, -mēn

# *Cultivate Interesting Hobbies*

It doesn't matter whether it's gardening, sewing, cooking, collecting Civil War books, buttons, or bottle tops. A hobby or interest requiring your disciplined concentration gets you out of yourself and into a world of activity that will add an extra dimension to your whole life.

*Best Friends*

. . . and how
to get them!

# Plan a Campaign

**Campaign Check List**

Let us make a "handy reference guide" for your campaign:

1. TOMORROW (the only "tomorrow" in your plans) is the start of your "I LIKE YOU" week.

2. For seven consecutive days you are going to let the world — your world — know about your slogan, "I LIKE YOU!"

3. You are going to set the stage each day, by being an "icebreaker" through your "get-acquainted" approach to people.

4. In succession, following your day-by-day "selling" program, you are going to use a different technique for winning friends.

First day — "Take the other person's viewpoint."
Second day — "Follow up on acquaintances."
Third day — "Ask a favor."
Fourth day — "Do a favor."
Fifth day — "Work together."
Sixth day — "Play together."
Seventh day — "Give recognition."

5. At the end of the week, you are going to add up your gains — which will be a *sizeable* list of friends.

**Have you been limiting yourself to one, best** **Friends lead to other friends and parties**

girlfriend? Don't drop her, but do branch out.

and that's what you're looking for, right?

# The popular girls. . .

*The popular girls always:*

Thoroughly enjoy the company of others.
Respect other's views and opinions.
Listen, but *really listen*, to what others have to say.
Are understanding and sympathetic.
Consider others at all times in all circumstances.
Have a good-natured and cheerful disposition.

*Never:*

Ask embarrassing questions.
Flaunt their knowledge or expensive possessions, if they have any.
Resent it if their opinions are not accepted.
Act affected or prudish, or think they are above others.
Lose their tempers.
Drop in to see anyone without an invitation.
Overstay their visit.

# *What Your Friends Won't Tell You*

**BODY ODOR IS OFFENSIVE** and an embarrassing state of being. And it is true that even your best friend won't tell you that you're not nice to be around because. . . . You needn't worry, however, if you use a good deodorant each morning and after every bath. A small jar may be bought for a nominal sum, so there is no excuse for any girl or boy to offend.

**TIP:** Sprinkle the ironing board with your favorite fragrance before pressing your date dress. It will absorb the scent and complement the matching perfume or spray that you're wearing on your skin.

Also, if the palms of your hands tend to get moist, dab a bit of anti-perspirant on them.

Nobody

ikes a gossip

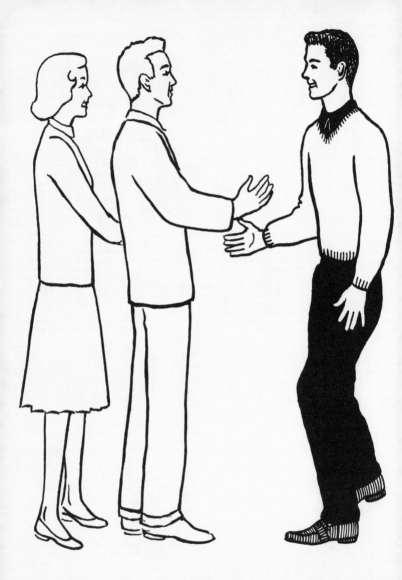

Do your traits that attract friends

outweigh those that repel them?

The Life of
the Party

. . . it's you!

# A hospitable welcome

# PARTY POPULARITY QUOTA

Here are some of the points to be considered that will add to your popularity quota:

1. *Invite your guests well in advance of the occasion . . . so that it does not conflict with other plans that they may have made.*

2. *Stimulate interest in your gatherings by adding a new face once in a while. The best friends can be bored with each other.*

3. *Rescue the shy guest. Keep your eyes open and draw them into conversation with others . . . or subtly persuade a friend to do so.*

4. *Act nonchalant if an invited guest attends with an unexpected and uninvited person.*

5. *Take it easy with new introductions. Don't get nervous and interrupt a conversation.*

6. *Don't carry your fussiness with the house to extreme. It will make the guests uneasy to see you fluff pillows and empty ash trays.*

# A drink — a must

**RUM PUNCH**

*(Serves about 30)*

*1¹/₂ Fifths Rum*
*6 Oz. Pineapple Juice*
*10 Oz. Orange Juice*
*10 Oz. Lemon Juice*
*1¹/₂ Large Bottles of Ginger Ale or Soda*

*Pour into a container and let steep for 1 hour. Add ginger ale or soda. Pour over block of ice in a punch bowl and stir. Decorate with pint of sliced strawberries, lemon and lime slices.*

## Ambrosia!

6 navel oranges
2 medium bananas

2 tablespoons sugar
½ cup grated coconut

Peel oranges and divide into sections. Place in a bowl and slice bananas into it. Add sugar and mix lightly. Chill. When ready to serve, top with coconut. Serves 8.

**DONUT STRING KISS STUNT** — At a special table, invite couples to compete with each other in a donut-eating contest. Provide them with a donut hung in the center of a string. The idea is that the man takes one end of the string in his mouth, the woman the other end in her mouth, and they both chew on the string rapidly to reach the donut in the center and eat it. The one who eats most of the donut is the winner. It will be a minor miracle if this little divertisement does not end in a kiss—to the amusement of onlookers—which is an appealing idea to young couples who are just looking for a good excuse anyhow.

## WALLFLOWER TEST

If you can honestly answer "Yes" to all these questions, you probably *won't* be a wallflower.

1. Can you dance a fox trot, one-step, waltz and at least two of the newer favorites such as: samba, rumba, conga, and jitterbug steps in moderation?

2. Do you know the names of the top tunes the orchestra will be playing and can you sing the words of at least three of the choruses?

3. Have you and your date something in common, such as an interest in sports, music, art, writing, so that you can carry on a good two-way conversation?

4. If your partner leaves you to dance with his sister or other girls, will there be others at the party you know well enough to talk to in case no one asks you to dance?

5. Have your mother and dad agreed that you are old enough to go on a real date?

It is very bad etiquette to exploit any of your guests by insisting that they entertain for your visitors. If they are talented, things will work out by themselves.

# Do's and Don'ts for Dancers

**Do** dance in the position that seems graceful to both you and your partner.

**Do** hold your partner gently but firmly.

**Do** make all motions naturally without any exaggeration.

**Do** learn to dance properly before accepting invitations.

**Do** look over your partner's right shoulder.

**Do** raise your feet for every step to the front, side, or rear.

**Do**, if you are a girl, learn the steps the man must make before going to dances.

**Do** keep your head and shoulders erect.

**Do** put the toes of your feet on the floor first, regardless of which direction you are going.

**Do** keep your entire leg, from the hip to the foot, in a straight line.

**Don't** get too close to your partner.

**Don't** dance too far away from your partner.

**Don't** go to dances until you can dance well.

**Don't** stare into your partner's face.

**Don't** pump your arms.

**Don't** make jerky motions—float along.

**Don't**, if you are tall, dance in an ugly posture to make yourself appear short.

**Don't**, if you are short, assume an uncomfortable posture trying to appear taller.

**Don't** wiggle your shoulders.

**Don't** bend your knees.

**Don't** dance on your toes.

**Don't** try bizarre holds.

**Don't** spread your feet apart.

**Don't** let your feet slide.

**Don't** crush your partner with a "bear hug."

＊

Always, repeat always, leave a party, dance or anything else with the same boy who brought you, no matter how groovy a guy you meet during the evening. There's always the next time for him—if he asks you.

True Love
. . . the most important
popularity of all!

Don't be afraid to start a conversation!

*Has every effort to get to know him failed? Okay, the next time you pass him, look him straight in the eye and in your friendliest but most ladylike tone of voice say, "Hi." Repeat, if necessary, but chances are before long he'll start considering you an already-acquaintance.*

# Guys

♥ Don't make her wait!

♥ Don't find fault. You can get used to an outlandish hat or purple lipstick.

♥ Don't have a roving eye!

♥ Don't brag about your amours.

♥ Don't make love in public.

♥ Don't tell her you love her just to be nice.

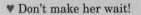

*Want to make him feel protective? Give yourself the "little girl look," and turn him into your knight in shining armor!*

# What about a bad reputation?

**SUPPOSE SOMETHING YOU ONCE DID WAS A SERIOUS MISTAKE**
What can you do about it? Perhaps in one mad, impulsive moment you got yourself into an awful mess. Can you ever live it down? If you have acquired a bad name from some person who in some way was linked with you, is there anything you can do to come out from under the shadow? These questions are not uncommon. They are usually best answered in the following ways.

**YOU MUST BE SURE YOU WANT TO**
The most important step in the process is to make up your own mind that you sincerely want to. If you have a secret enjoyment of your shady reputation and the things that caused it, the chances are you will not be successful in shaking them off. As soon as you have definitely decided that you want to follow a different practice, you are free to start moving in that direction.

**BEND OVER BACKWARDS FOR A WHILE**
Whatever you did (or were supposed to have done) that offended your conscience or your reputation in the first place must be avoided if you are to clear up your mind about it, and you reputation with others (if they know of it). You must bend over backwards and be more careful if you are in the process of cleaning up a habit or reputation.

# Credits

**p. 1:** Illustration from *Teen Magazine*, 1964. **pp. 2–3:** Illustration from *The Nancy Taylor Course Book II* by Nancy Taylor, Flower Lane Publishing Company, Inc., 1958, 1962. **pp. 4–5:** Illustrations from *Murray-Go-Round*, Arthur Murray, Inc., 1967. **pp. 6–7:** Illustration from *So You Want to Be Popular* by Fayly H. Cothern. Copyright © 1960 by Zondervan Publishing House. Used by permission of Zondervan. **pp. 8–9:** Illustration from CSA Images. **pp. 10–11:** Illustration from *Couples Clip Book of Line Art*, Harry Volk Jr. Art Studio, 1965. Reprinted with the permission of Dynamic Graphics, Inc. **pp. 12–13:** "Of course you want to be popular" from *Hi There, High School!* by Gay Head, Scholastic Company, 1953. Reprinted with the permission of Scholastic, Inc. Illustration from *Teen-Time Cooking with Carnation* by Mary Blake, Carnation Company, 1959. **pp. 14–15:** Illustrations from *Thresholds to Adult Living* by Hazel Thompson Craig, Chas. A. Bennett Co., Inc., 1962. "It Matters Very Much" from *100 Ways to Popularity* by Joan O'Sullivan, Ace Books, Inc. by arrangement with The Macmillan Company, 1963. **pp. 16–17:** "One can never improve" from *So You Want to Be Popular* by Fayly H. Cothern. Copyright © 1960 by Zondervan Publishing House. Used by permission of Zondervan. Illustration from *Concepts in Clothing* by Judy Lynn Graef and Joan Buesher Strom, illustrated by Craven & Evans; Meredith Nemirov; Jack Weaver; Graphic Arts International; Vantage Art, Webster Division, McGraw-Hill Book Company, 1976. **pp. 18–19:** Illustration from *Teen Scene–1001 Groovy Hints & Tips* by Milburn Smith and Rochelle Larkin, illustrated by Jane Thornton Banci, Pyramid Books, 1970. Illustration from Metro Associated Services, Inc., 1969. **pp. 20–21:** "Popularity is like a tree" from *Teen-Age Popularity and Manners* by Marjorie Ellis McCrady, T. S. Denison & Company, Inc., 1964. Cheerleader illustration from *Summer Clip Book of Line Art*, Volk Corporation, 1973. Reprinted with the permission of Dynamic Graphics, Inc. **pp. 22–23:** Illustration from *The ABC's of Beauty* by Barbara Marco, illustrated by Jacqueline Kingsbury, Macfadden-Bartell Corporation, 1963. **pp. 24–25:** Illustrations from *Women Clip Book of Line Art*, Volk Corporation, 1973. Reprinted with the permission of Dynamic Graphics, Inc. "Science makes you more beautiful" from *A Guide to Better Living* compiled and edited by N. H. and S. K. Mager, Affiliated Publishers, Inc., 1957. **pp. 26–27:** Illustration from *The Life Cycle Library for Young People, Book 4 Glossary and Index*, Parent and Child Institute, 1969. Illustration from *Teen-Age Glamor* by Adah Broadbent, illustrated by Anna Marie Magagna, Doubleday & Company, Inc., 1955. "Everyday" from *Taffy's Tips to Teens* by Dolly Martin, Grosset & Dunlap by arrangement with Prentice-Hall, Inc., 1968. Brushing hair illustration from *Personality Unlimited* by Veronica Dengel, illustrated by Sylvia Haggander, The John C. Winston Company, 1943. **pp. 28–29:** Illustrations from *Summer Clip Book of Line Art*, Volk Corporation, 1973. Reprinted with the permission of Dynamic Graphics, Inc. "Sun fun" from *Teen Scene–1001 Groovy Hints & Tips* by Milburn Smith and Rochelle Larkin, illustrated by Jane Thornton Banci, Pyramid Books, 1970. **pp. 30–31:** Illustrations from *Concepts in Clothing* by Judy Lynn Graef and Joan Buesher Strom, illustrated by Craven & Evans; Meredith Nemirov; Jack Weaver; Graphic Arts International; Vantage Art, Webster Division, McGraw-Hill Book Company, 1976. "The following physical traits" from *How to Improve Your Personality* by Earl Lockhart, Walton Publishing Company, 1941. **pp. 32–33:** Illustration from *Women Clip Book of*

*Line Art*, Volk Corporation, 1973. Reprinted with the permission of Dynamic Graphics, Inc. "The hippest closet in town" from *Teen Scene—1001 Groovy Hints & Tips* by Milburn Smith and Rochelle Larkin, illustrated by Jane Thornton Banci, Pyramid Books, 1970. Illustration from Metro Associated Services, Inc., 1969. **pp. 34–35:** Illustration from *Concepts in Clothing* by Judy Lynn Graef and Joan Buesher Strom, illustrated by Craven & Evans; Merideth Nemirov; Jack Weaver; Graphic Arts International; Vantage Art, Webster Division, McGraw-Hill Book Company, 1976. **pp. 36–37:** "Research shows that if you wear certain" from *The Woman's Dress for Success Book* by John T. Molloy, Reardon & Walsh, a subsidiary of Summit Press Syndicate and Follett Publishing Company, 1977. Illustration from *Concepts in Clothing* by Judy Lynn Graef and Joan Buesher Strom, illustrated by Craven & Evans; Merideth Nemirov; Jack Weaver; Graphic Arts International; Vantage Art, Webster Division, McGraw-Hill Book Company, 1976. **pp. 38–39:** "Tired of counting" from *Teen Scene—1001 Groovy Hints & Tips* by Milburn Smith and Rochelle Larkin, illustrated by Jane Thornton Banci, Pyramid Books, 1970. Illustration from *Total Beauty* by DuBarry, Inc., 1972, prepared by Western Publishing Company, Inc. **pp. 40–41:** Illustration from *The Life Cycle Library for Young People, Book 4 Glossary and Index*, Parent and Child Institute, 1969. "If you want to breathe easy" from *100 Ways to Popularity* by Joan O'Sullivan, Ace Books, Inc. by arrangement with The Macmillan Company, 1963. **pp. 42–43:** Illustration from *Molloy's Live for Success* by John T. Molloy, Bantam Books in association with William Morrow and Company, Inc., 1981. Illustration from Metro Associated Services, Inc., 1968. **pp. 44–45:** Illustration from *The Nancy Taylor Course Book II* by Nancy Taylor, Flower Lane Publishing Company, Inc., 1958. Illustration from *Personality Unlimited* by Veronica Dengel, illustrated by Sylvia Haggander, The John C. Winston Company, 1943. **pp. 46–47:** Illustration from Clipper Creative Art Service, Dynamic Graphics, Inc. Reprinted with the permission of Dynamic Graphics, Inc. "Your eyes are the most important part" from *P.S. for Private Secretaries: The Secretary's Guide to Beauty and Charm*, Vol. 5 No. 4, February 25, 1962, Bureau of Business Practice, a division of Prentice-Hall, Inc., 1962. **pp. 48–49:** Illustration from Clipper Creative Art Service, Dynamic Graphics, Inc. Reprinted with the permission of Dynamic Graphics, Inc. **pp. 50–51:** Illustration from *The Life Cycle Library for Young People, Book 4 Glossary and Index*, Parent and Child Institute, 1969. Illustration from *Graphic Source Clip Art: Family and Youth*, Graphic Products Corporation, 1986. "Have confidence in yourself" from *100 Ways to Popularity* by Joan O'Sullivan, Ace Books, Inc. by arrangement with The Macmillan Company, 1963. **pp. 52–53:** Illustration from *Couples Clip Book of Line Art*, Volk Corporation, 1973. Reprinted with the permission of Dynamic Graphics, Inc. "Assets of Enthusiasm" from *How to Develop a Million Dollar Personality* by J. V. Cerney, Castle Books, 1964. Cheerleader illustration from Metro Associated Services, Inc., 1967. **pp. 54–55:** Illustration from *Personal Adjustment, Marriage, and Family Living* by Judson T. Landis and Mary G. Landis. Copyright © 1950, 1955, 1960, by Prentice-Hall, Inc.; copyright renewed © 1978, 1983, 1988 by Judson T. Landis and Mary G. Landis. Reprinted with the permission of Simon & Schuster Adult Publishing Group. **pp. 56–57:** Illustration from Metro Associated Services, Inc., 1969. "Testing yourself for charm" from *How to Win Your Man and Keep Him* by Jean and Eugene Benge,

Windsor Press, 1948. **pp. 58–59:** Illustration from *Molloy's Live for Success* by John T. Molloy, Bantam Books in association with William Morrow and Company, Inc. 1981. **pp. 60–61:** Illustration from *The Life Cycle Library for Young People, Book 4 Glossary and Index,* Parent and Child Institute, 1969. "The antonym for humility" from *So You Want to Be Popular* by Fayly H. Cothern. Copyright © 1960 by Zondervan Publishing House. Illustration from Kandel Knits, Inc., 1970. **pp. 62–63:** "Here is a short test" from *Thresholds to Adult Living* by Hazel Thompson Craig, Chas. A. Bennett Co., Inc., 1962. Illustration from Picto-Cabulary Series: *Stubby Beards & Gaunt Faces* by Richard A. Boning, Barnell Loft, Ltd., 1971. **pp. 64–65:** Illustrations from *Office Clip Book of Line Art,* Volk Corporation, 1973. Reprinted with the permission of Dynamic Graphics, Inc. "Avoid these harmful personality traits" from *How to Improve Your Personality* by Earl Lockhart, Walton Publishing Company, 1941. **pp. 66–67:** Illustrations from *Office Clip Book of Line Art,* Volk Corporation. Reprinted with the permission of Dynamic Graphics, Inc. "Be a person on whom others can depend" from *The New American Etiquette* by Lily Haxworth Wallace, Books, Inc., 1941. **pp. 68–69:** Illustration from *Graphic Source Clip Art: Family and Youth,* Graphic Products Corporation, 1986. "Your voice is your instrument" from *100 Ways to Popularity* by Joan O'Sullivan, Ace Books, Inc. by arrangement with The Macmillan Company, 1963. "If possible, make tape recordings" from *Thresholds to Adult Living* by Hazel Thompson Craig, Chas. A. Bennett Co., Inc., 1962. Illustration from *Clip Art Book,* Lifetouch Publishing, 1991. **pp. 70–71:** Illustration from *Develop Your Leadership Potential* by Shon Ross, Employee Communications, Inc., 1976. "You certainly do not need an over-cultivated" from *Develop Your Leadership Potential* by Shon Ross, Employee Communications, Inc., 1976. **pp. 72–73:** "How's Your Speech" from *Personality Unlimited* by Veronica Dengel, The John C. Winston Company, 1943. **pp. 74–75:** Illustration from *International Visual Dictionary* by Leo Francis Daniels, illustrated by Fernando Burgos Perez, Clute International Institute, 1973. "It doesn't matter whether it's gardening" from *The Amy Vanderbilt Success Program For Women: How to Be a More Interesting Woman* by Barbara Wedgwood, Nelson Doubleday, Inc., 1965. Illustration from *You and Your Job* by Henry Brandt, Scripture Press Publications, Inc., 1966. **pp. 76–77:** Illustration from *Couples Clip Book of Line Art,* Volk Corporation, 1973. Reprinted with the permission of Dynamic Graphics, Inc. **pp. 78–79:** "Plan a Campaign" from *How to Improve Your Personality In Just 15 Minutes a Day* By Charles Simmons and Charles Simmons II, P & B Publishing Company, 1962. Illustration from *Office Clip Book of Line Art,* Volk Corporation, 1973. Reprinted with the permission of Dynamic Graphics, Inc. **pp. 80–81:** Illustration from *Women Clip Book of Line Art,* Volk Corporation, 1973. Reprinted with the permission of Dynamic Graphics, Inc. "Have you been limiting yourself" from *Teen Scene–1001 Groovy Hints & Tips* by Milburn Smith and Rochelle Larkin, illustrated by Jane Thornton Banci, Pyramid Books, 1970. **pp. 82–83:** "The popular girls" from *Taffy's Tips to Teens* by Dolly Martin, Grosset & Dunlap by arrangement with Prentice-Hall, Inc., 1968. Illustration from *You're Entertaining: America's Junior Miss Party Guide,* Home Service Center, Scott Paper Company, 1965. **pp. 84–85:** Illustration from *The Nancy Taylor Course Book II* by Nancy Taylor, Flower Lane Publishing Company, Inc., 1962. "Body odor is offensive" from *So You Want to Be Popular* by Fayly H. Cothern. Copyright © 1960 by Zondervan Publishing House. "Sprinkle the ironing board" from *Teen Scene–1001 Groovy Hints & Tips* by Milburn Smith and Rochelle Larkin, illustrated by Jane Thornton Banci, Pyramid Books, 1970. **pp. 86–87:** Illustrations from *So You Want to Be Popular* by Fayly H. Cothern. Copyright

© 1960 by Zondervan Publishing House. Used by permission of Zondervan. **pp. 88–89:** Illustration from *Thresholds to Adult Living* by Hazel Thompson Craig, Chas. A. Bennett Co., Inc., 1962. **pp. 90–91:** Illustration from *Graphic Source Clip Art: Family and Youth*, Graphic Products Corporation, 1986. **pp. 92–93:** Illustration from *Thresholds to Adult Living* by Hazel Thompson Craig, Chas. A. Bennett Co., Inc., 1962. **pp. 94–95:** Illustration from *Easy-Do Parties Electrically*, Milliken Publishing Company, 1960. "Here are some points to be considered" from *How to Become a More Popular Hostess* by Joe Bonomo, Bonomo Culture Institute, Inc., 1954. **pp. 96–97:** "Rum punch" from *The Calvert Party Encyclopedia: Your Complete Guide to Home Entertainment*, Calvert Distillers Company, no date. Illustration from *Easy-Do Parties Electrically*, Milliken Publishing Company, 1960. **pp. 98–99:** Illustration from *Teen-Time Cooking with Carnation* by Mary Blake, Carnation Company, 1959. "Ambrosia" from *The Amy Vanderbilt Success Program For Women: How to Prepare Exciting Holiday Menus* by Charlotte Adams, Nelson Doubleday, Inc., 1964. "Donut String Kiss" from *How to Run a Successful Party*, Doughnut Corp. of America, 1945. **pp. 100–101:** Illustration by Ron Wolin from *Teen Magazine*, June 1969. "Wallflower test" from *The Teen-Age Manual* by Edith Heal, Pocket Books, 1948. **pp. 102–103:** Illustrations from *Physical Education for Life* by Charles A. Bucher, Webster Division, McGraw-Hill Book Company, 1969. "It is very bad etiquette" from *How to Become a More Popular Hostess* by Joe Bonomo, Bonomo Culture Institute, Inc., 1954. **pp. 104–105:** "Do's and Don'ts" from *The New American Etiquette* by Lily Haxworth Wallace, Books, Inc., 1941. Illustration from Metro Associated Services, Inc., 1969. **pp. 106–107:** Illustration from *Couples Clip Book of Line Art*, Volk Corporation, 1973. Reprinted with the permission of Dynamic Graphics, Inc. "Always, repeat always" from *Teen Scene–1001 Groovy Hints & Tips* by Milburn Smith and Rochelle Larkin, illustrated by Jane Thornton Banci, Pyramid Books, 1970. **pp. 108–109:** Illustration from Dynamic Graphics, Inc. Reprinted with the permission of Dynamic Graphics, Inc. **pp. 110–111:** Illustration from *Teen-Time Cooking with Carnation* by Mary Blake, Carnation Company, 1959. **pp. 112–113:** Illustration from *Summer Clip Book of Line Art*, Volk Corporation, 1973. Reprinted with the permission of Dynamic Graphics, Inc. "Has every effort to get to know him failed?" from *Teen Scene–1001 Groovy Hints & Tips* by Milburn Smith and Rochelle Larkin, illustrated by Jane Thornton Banci, Pyramid Books, 1970. **pp. 114–115:** "Don't make her wait" from *How to Get Along with Girls* by Walter S. Keating, Stravon Publishers, 1944. Illustration from *Summer Clip Book of Line Art*, Volk Corporation, 1973. Reprinted with the permission of Dynamic Graphics, Inc. **pp. 116–117:** Illustration from *International Visual Dictionary* by Leo Francis Daniels, illustrated by Fernando Burgos Perez, Clute International Institute, 1973. Illustration from *Women Clip Book of Line Art*, Volk Corporation, 1973. Reprinted with the permission of Dynamic Graphics, Inc. "Want to make him feel protective" from *Teen Scene–1001 Groovy Hints & Tips* by Milburn Smith and Rochelle Larkin, illustrated by Jane Thornton Banci, Pyramid Books, 1970. **pp. 118–119:** Illustration from *Ms. Clip Book of Line Art*, Volk Corporation, 1973. "Suppose something you once did" from *Facts of Life And Love for Teenagers* by Evelyn Millis Duvall, Popular Library, published by arrangement with Association Press, 1950. **pp. 120–123:** Illustration from Clip Art Book, Lifetouch Publishing, 1991. **pp. 124–125:** Illustration from *Graphic Source Clip Art: Family and Youth*, Graphic Products Corporation, 1986.